YOUR KNOWLEDGE HAS VALUE

- We will publish your bachelor's and master's thesis, essays and papers

- Your own eBook and book - sold worldwide in all relevant shops

- Earn money with each sale

Upload your text at www.GRIN.com and publish for free

Hardik Modi

Digital Signal Processing Laboratory Experiments using MATLAB

LAB Manual

GRIN Verlag

Bibliografische Information der Deutschen Nationalbibliothek:

Die Deutsche Bibliothek verzeichnet diese Publikation in der Deutschen National-
bibliografie; detaillierte bibliografische Daten sind im Internet über http://dnb.d-
nb.de/ abrufbar.

Imprint:

Copyright © 2014 GRIN Verlag GmbH
Druck und Bindung: Books on Demand GmbH, Norderstedt Germany
ISBN: 978-3-656-62141-6

This book at GRIN:

http://www.grin.com/en/e-book/270625/digital-signal-processing-laboratory-expe-
riments-using-matlab

GRIN - Your knowledge has value

Der GRIN Verlag publiziert seit 1998 wissenschaftliche Arbeiten von Studenten, Hochschullehrern und anderen Akademikern als eBook und gedrucktes Buch. Die Verlagswebsite www.grin.com ist die ideale Plattform zur Veröffentlichung von Hausarbeiten, Abschlussarbeiten, wissenschaftlichen Aufsätzen, Dissertationen und Fachbüchern.

Visit us on the internet:

http://www.grin.com/

http://www.facebook.com/grincom

http://www.twitter.com/grin_com

Digital Signal Processing Laboratory Experiments using MATLAB

List of Experiments

Exp. No	Name of Experiment
1	To represent basic signals like:Unit Impulse, Ramp, Unit Step, Exponential.
2	To generate discrete sine and cosine signals with given sampling frequency.
3	To represent complex exponential as a function of real and imaginary part.
4	To determine impulse and step response of two vectors using MATLAB.
5	To perform convolution between two vectors using MATLAB.
6	To perform cross correlation between two vectors using MATLAB.
7	To compute DFT and IDFT of a given sequence using MATLAB.
8	To perform linear convolution of two sequence using DFT using MATLAB.
9	To determine z-transform from the given transfer function and its ROC using MATLAB.
10	To determine rational z-transform from the given poles and zeros using MATLAB.
11	To determine partial fraction expansion of rational z-transform using MATLAB. $$H(z) = \frac{18z^3}{18z^3+3z^2-4z-1}$$
12	To design a Type 1 Chebyshev IIR highpass filter using MATLAB.
13	To design an IIR Elliptic low pass filter using MATLAB.
14	To design an IIR Butterworth bandpass filter using MATLAB.
15	To generate rectangular ,hamming ,hanning ,blackman and kaier window using MATLAB.
16	To design low pass filter using the Kaiser window using MATLAB.
17	To study coefficient quantization effects on the frequency response of a cascade form IIR filter using MATLAB.

DIGITAL SIGNAL PROCESSING

EXPERIMENT – 1

AIM : To represent basic signals like
1. Unit Impulse
2. Ramp
3. Unit Step
4. Exponential.

PROGRAM :

```
clc;
clear all;
t=0:1:10;

y = [zeros(1,5),ones(1,1),zeros(1,5)];      %%Unit Impulse Signal
subplot(2,2,1);
stem(t,y);
xlabel('Unit Impulse');
ylabel('Amplitude');

y = 0:1:10;                                  %% Ramp Signal
subplot(2,2,2);
stem(t,y);
xlabel('Ramp');
ylabel('Amplitude');

y = ones(1,11);                              %% Unit Step Signal
subplot(2,2,3);
stem(t,y);
xlabel('Unit Step');
ylabel('Amplitude');

y = exp(t);                                  %% Exponential Signal
subplot(2,2,4);
stem(t,y);
xlabel('Exponential');
ylabel('Amplitude');
```

DIGITAL SIGNAL PROCESSING

GRAPHS :

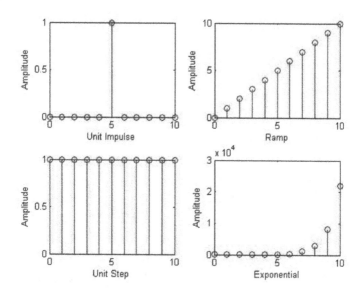

CONCLUSION :
      From this experiment we can conclude that we can observe the waveforms of basic signals using MATLAB.

EXPERIMENT – 2

AIM : To generate discrete sine and cosine signals with given sampling frequency.

PROGRAM :

```
clc;
clear all;

fs = input('Enter sampling frequency:');
f = input('Enter signal frequency:');
a = input('Enter amplitude:');

t = 0:(1/fs):1;                          %%Generation of SINE signal
y = a*sin(2*pi*f*t);
subplot(2,1,1);
stem(t,y);
xlabel('Time --------→');
ylabel('Amplitude --------→');
title('Sine Wave');

t = 0:(1/fs):1;                          %%Generation of COSINE signal
y = a*cos(2*pi*f*t);
subplot(2,1,2);
stem(t,y);
xlabel('Time --------→');
ylabel('Amplitude --------→');
title('Cosine Wave');
```

INPUT :

Enter sampling frequency: 40
Enter signal frequency: 2
Enter amplitude: 2

GRAPHS :

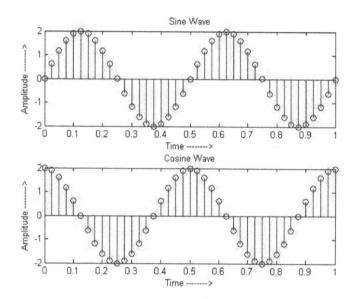

CONCLUSION :
From this experiment we can generate discrete sine and cosine signal with given sampling frequency using MATLAB.

DIGITAL SIGNAL PROCESSING

EXPERIMENT – 3

AIM : To represent complex exponential as a function of real and imaginary part.

PROGRAM :

```
clc;
clear all;

a = input('Enter real value');
b = input('Enter imaginary value');
k = input('Enter gain');
n = input('Enter length of sequence');

t = 0:1:n;                              %%Exponential Graph
c = a+(i*b);
y = k*exp(c*t);
subplot(3,1,1);
stem(t,y);
xlabel('Time --------→');
ylabel('Amplitude --------→');
title('Exponential Graph');

x = real(y);                            %%Real part of Exponential graph
subplot(3,1,2);
stem(t,x);
xlabel('Time --------→');
ylabel('Amplitude --------→');
title('Real Part');

z = imag(y);                            %%Imaginary part of Exponential graph
subplot(3,1,3);
stem(t,z);
xlabel('Time --------→');
ylabel('Amplitude --------→');
title('Imaginary Part');
```

INPUT :

Enter real value: 1/12
Enter imaginary value: pi/6
Enter gain: 2
Enter length of sequence: 40

GRAPHS :

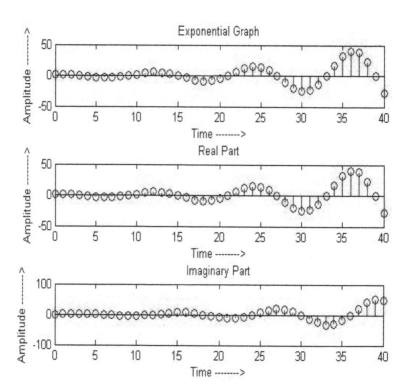

CONCLUSION :
From this experiment we can represent complex exponential as a function of real and imaginary part using MATLAB.

DIGITAL SIGNAL PROCESSING

EXPERIMENT – 4

AIM : To determine impulse and step response of two vectors using MATLAB.

PROGRAM :

```
clc;
clear all;

n = input('Enter sequence:');
p = input('Enter value of P:');
d = input('Enter value of D:');

y = [ones(1,1),zeros(1,n-1)];          %%Impulse response
f = filter(p,d,y);
subplot(2,1,1);
stem(f);
xlabel('Time -------->');
ylabel('Amplitude -------->');
title('Impulse response');

y = [ones(1,n)];                       %%Step response
f = filter(p,d,y);
subplot(2,1,2);
stem(f);
xlabel('Time -------->');
ylabel('Amplitude -------->');
title('Step response');
```

9

DIGITAL SIGNAL PROCESSING

INPUT :

Enter sequence: 20
Enter value of P: [0.8 -0.44 0.36 0.02]
Enter value of D: [1 0.7 -0.45 -0.6]

GRAPHS :

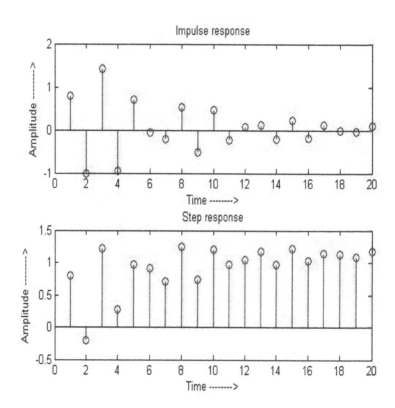

CONCLUSION :

From this experiment we can determine impulse and step response of two
vectors using MATLAB.

EXPERIMENT – 5

AIM : To perform convolution between two vectors using MATLAB.

PROGRAM :

```
clc;
clear all;

a = input('Enter a --→');
b = input('Enter b --→');
m = conv(a,b);                    %%For convolution between a and b
stem(m);
xlabel('Time --------→');
ylabel('Amplitude --------→');
title('Convolution between two vectors');
```

INPUT :

Enter a --→[1 4 5 6]
Enter b --→[2 7 5 6]

GRAPH :

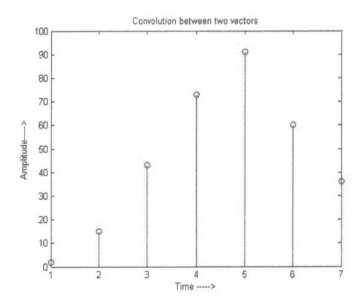

CONCLUSION :
From this experiment we can perform convolution between two vectors using MATLAB.

DIGITAL SIGNAL PROCESSING

EXPERIMENT – 6

AIM : To perform cross correlation between two vectors using MATLAB.

PROGRAM :

```
clc;
clear all;

a = input('Enter a --→');
b = input('Enter b --→');
m = xcorr(a,b);                          %%For cross correlation between a and b
stem(m);
xlabel('Time --------→');
ylabel('Amplitude --------→');
title('Cross Correlation between two vectors');
```

INPUT :

Enter a --→[1 4 5 6]
Enter b --→[2 7 5 6]

GRAPH :

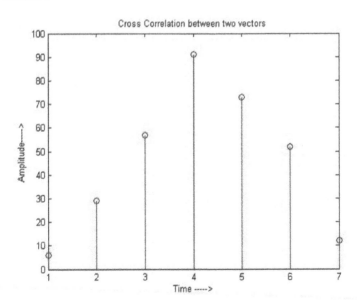

13

CONCLUSION :
From this experiment we can perform cross correlation between two vectors using MATLAB.

EXPERIMENT – 7

AIM : To compute DFT and IDFT of a given sequence using MATLAB.

PROGRAM :

%DFT COMPUTATION

```
clc;
clear all;
N=input('Length of Sequence');
M=input('Length of DFT');
k=0:1:M-1;
x=[ones(1,N)];

y = fft(x,M);                          %DFT of given sequence
subplot(2,3,1);
stem(y);
xlabel('Time ----->');
ylabel('Amplitude----->');

z=abs(y);
subplot(2,3,2);
stem(z);
xlabel('Time ----->');
ylabel('Amplitude----->');

a=unwrap(angle(y));
subplot(2,3,3);
stem(a);
xlabel('Time ----->');
ylabel('Amplitude----->');
```

DIGITAL SIGNAL PROCESSING

GRAPH :

1. DFT of the given sequence.
2. Magnitude of DFT.
3. Phase of DFT.

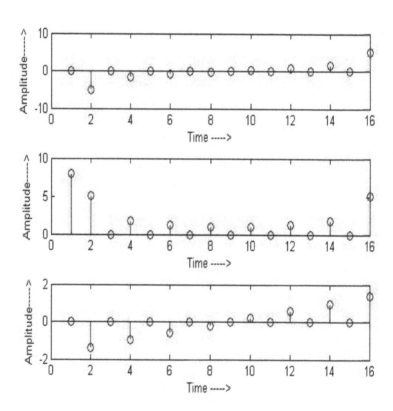

PROGRAM :

%IDFT COPMPUTATION

```
clc;
clear all;
N=input('Length of Sequence');
M=input('Length of DFT');
k=0:1:M-1;
x=[ones(1,N)];

b=ifft(x,M);                          %IDFT of given sequence
subplot(3,1,1);
stem(b);
xlabel('Time ----->');
ylabel('Amplitude----->');

c=abs(b);
subplot(3,1,2);
stem(c);
xlabel('Time ----->');
ylabel('Amplitude----->');

d=unwrap(angle(b));
subplot(3,1,3);
stem(d);
xlabel('Time ----->');
ylabel('Amplitude----->');
```

DIGITAL SIGNAL PROCESSING

GRAPH :

1. IDFT of the given sequence.
2. Magnitude of IDFT.
3. Phase of IDFT.

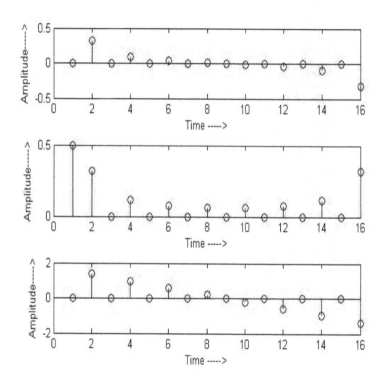

CONCLUSION :

        From this experiment we can compute DFT and IDFT of a given sequence using MATLAB.

EXPERIMENT – 8

AIM : To perform linear convolution of two sequence using DFT using MATLAB.

PROGRAM :

```
clc;
clear all;
g=input('Enter the first sequence');
h=input('Enter the second sequence');
l=length(g)+length(h)-1;

ge=fft(g,l);            %compute DFT by zero padding
he=fft(h,l);

y=ifft(ge.*he);         %determine IDFT
subplot(2,1,1);         %DFT based convolution
stem(y);
xlabel('Time ----->');
ylabel('Amplitude----->');
title('DFT based convolution');

a=conv(g,h);            %error from direct convolution
diff=y-a;
b=abs(diff);
subplot(2,1,2);
stem(b);
xlabel('Time ----->');
ylabel('Amplitude----->');
title('Error signal');
```

INPUT :

Enter the first sequence[1 2 4 6 8]
Enter the second sequence[1 3 5 7 9]

GRAPHS :

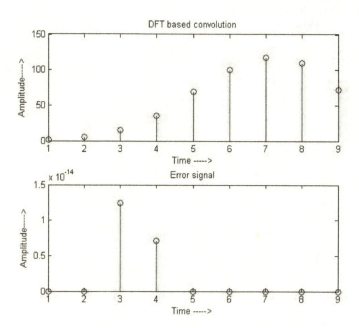

CONCLUSION :
   From this experiment we can perform linear convolution of two sequence using DFT using MATLAB.

DIGITAL SIGNAL PROCESSING

EXPERIMENT – 9

AIM : To determine z-transform from the given transfer function and its ROC using MATLAB.

PROGRAM :

```
clc;
clear all;
b = input('Enter numerator value : ');
a = input('Enter denominator value : ')
[b,a] = eqtflength(b,a);
[z,p,k] = tf2zp(b,a);          %transfer function to z-transform
disp(z');
disp(p');
disp(k);
m=abs(p);                       %ROC
disp(m');
sos = zp2sos(z,p,k);            %second-order section
disp(sos);
zplane(b,a);
```

INPUT :

Enter numerator value : [2 16 44 56 32]
Enter denominator value : [3 3 15 18 -12]

OUTPUT :
Zeros:
-4.0000   -2.0000   -1.0000 - 1.0000i -1.0000 + 1.0000i

Poles:
0.0203 - 2.3956i 0.0203 + 2.3956i -1.5040   0.4634

Gain:
0.6667

Radius of poles:
2.3957   2.3957   1.5040   0.4634

Range:
2.3957< |z|<= infinity
1.5040<|z|<2.3957
0.4634<|z|<1.5040
0.0000<=|z|<0.4634

21

Second-order section:
```
0.6667   4.0000   5.3333   1.0000   1.0405   -0.6970
1.0000   2.0000   2.0000   1.0000  -0.0405    5.7391
```

GRAPH :

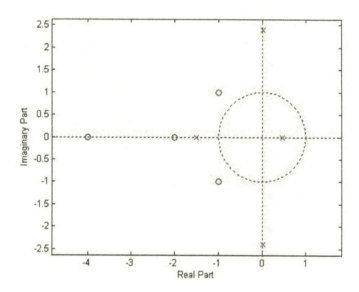

CONCLUSION :
　　　　From this experiment we can determine z-transform of given transfer function and its ROC using MATLAB.

DIGITAL SIGNAL PROCESSING

EXPERIMENT – 10

AIM : To determine rational z-transform from the given poles and zeros using MATLAB.

PROGRAM :

```
clc;
clear all;
zr=input('Enter the values of zeros :');
pr=input('Enter the values of poles :');
k=input('Enter the value of gain :');
z=zr';
p=pr';
[b,a]=zp2tf(z,p,k);          %rational z-transform
disp(a);
disp(b);
zplane(b,a);
```

INPUT :

Enter the values of zeros : [0.21 3.14 -0.3+0.5j -0.3-0.5j]
Enter the values of poles : [0.45 0.69 0.81+0.72j 0.81-0.72j]
Enter the value of gain :2.2

OUTPUT :

Polynomial coefficients:-

Numerator:
2.2000 -6.0500 -2.2233 -1.6354   0.4932

Denominator:
1.0000 -2.7600   3.3318 -1.8419   0.3647

$$H(z) = \frac{2.2z^4 - 6.05z^3 - 2.2233z^2 - 1.6354z + 0.4932}{z^4 - 2.76z^3 + 3.3318z^2 - 1.8419z + 0.3647}$$

23

GRAPH :

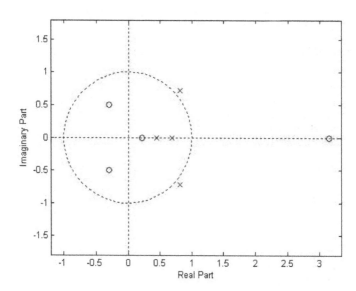

CONCLUSION :

From this experiment we can determine rational z-transform of given poles and zeros using MATLAB.

EXPERIMENT – 11

AIM : To determine partial fraction expansion of rational z-transform using MATLAB.

$$H(z) = \frac{18z^3}{18z^3 + 3z^2 - 4z - 1}$$

PROGRAM :

```
clc;
clear all;
b = input('Enter numerator value : ');
a = input('Enter denominator value : ');
[r,p,k]=residuez(b,a);                    %partial fraction expansion
disp(r');
disp(p');
disp(k');
```

INPUT :

Enter numerator value : [18 0 0 0]
Enter denominator value : [18 3 -4 -1]

OUTPUT :

Residues:
0.3600   0.2400   0.4000

Poles:
0.5000   -0.3333   -0.3333

Constant:
0

$$\frac{b(z)}{a(z)} = \frac{0.36}{1-0.5z^{-1}} + \frac{0.24}{(1+0.33z^{-1})^2} + \frac{0.4}{(1+0.33z^{-1})^2}$$

CONCLUSION :

Form this experiment we can determine partial fraction expansion of rational z-transform using MATLAB.

EXPERIMENT – 12

AIM : To design a Type 1 Chebyshev IIR highpass filter using MATLAB.

PROGRAM :

```
clc;
clear all;
Wp = input('Enter normalized passband edge in Hz :');
Ws = input('Enter normalized stopband edge in Hz :');
Rp = input('Enter passband ripple in dB :');
Rs = input('Enter stopband attenuation in dB :');
Ft = input('Enter sampling rate in Hz:');
[n,Wn] = cheb1ord(Wp,Ws,Rp,Rs);
[b,a] = cheby1(n,Rp,Wn,'high');
[h,w] = freqz(b,a,256);          %filter's frequency response
plot(w/pi,20*log(10*abs(h)));
grid;
xlabel('w/\pi');
ylabel('Gain,dB');
title('TYPE 1 CHEBYSHEV IIR HIGHPASS FILTER');
```

INPUT :
Enter normalized passband edge in Hz :0.7
Enter normalized stopband edge in Hz :0.5
Enter passband ripple in dB :1
Enter stopband attenuation in dB :32
Enter sampling rate in Hz:2

GRAPH :

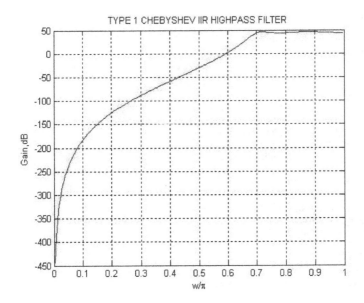

CONCLUSION :
From this experiment we can design a Type 1 Chebyshev IIR highpass filter which can block a low frequence impulse signal below attenuation level of 0.6dB.

ING

EXPERIMENT – 13

AIM : To design an IIR Elliptic low pass filter using MATLAB.

PROGRAM :

```
clc;
clear all;
Fp = input('Enter pass edge frequency :');
Fs = input('Enter stop edge frequency :');
Rp = input('Enter ripple in passband :');
Rs = input('Enter stopband attenuation :');
Ft = input('Enter sampling rate :');
Wp = 2*pi*(Fp/Ft);
Ws = 2*pi*(Fs/Ft);
[n,Wn] = ellipord(Wp,Ws,Rp,Rs);
[b,a] = ellip(n,Rp,Rs,Wn);
[h,w] = freqz(b,a,256);                    %filter's frequency response
plot(w/pi,20*log(10*abs(h)));
grid;
xlabel('w/\pi');
ylabel('Gain,dB');
title('IIR ELLIPTIC LOWPASS FILTER');
```

INPUT :
Enter pass edge frequency : 800
Enter stop edge frequency : 1000
Enter ripple in passband : 0.5
Enter stopband attenuation : 40
Enter sampling rate :8000

28

GRAPH :

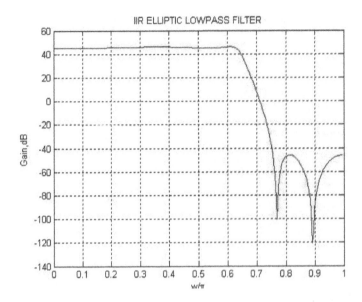

CONCLUSION :
      From this experiment we can design an IIR elliptic low pass filter which can block a high frequence impulse signal at attenuation level of 0.5dB.

EXPERIMENT – 14

AIM : To design an IIR Butterworth bandpass filter using MATLAB.

PROGRAM :

```
clc;
clear all;
Wp = input('Enter normalized passband edge  :');
Ws = input('Enter normalized stopband edge :');
Rp = input('Enter passband ripple in dB :');
Rs = input('Enter stopband attenuation in dB :');
[n,Wn] = buttord(Wp,Ws,Rp,Rs);
[b,a] = butter(n,Rp,Wn,'high');
[h,w] = freqz(b,a,256);        %filter's frequency response
plot(w/pi,20*log(10*abs(h)));
grid;
xlabel('w/\pi');
ylabel('Gain,dB');
title('IIR BUTTERWORTH BANDPASS FILTER');
```

INPUT :

Enter normalized passband edge :[0.45 0.65]
Enter normalized stopband edge :[0.3 0.75]
Enter passband ripple in dB :1
Enter stopband attenuation in dB :40

GRAPH :

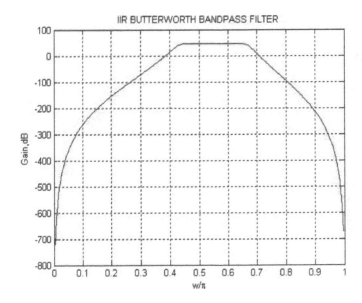

CONCLUSION :
From this experiment we can design an IIR Butterworth bandpass filter which can allow a band of frequencies between attenuation levels of 0.3dB to 0.8dB.

DIGITAL SIGNAL PROCESSING

EXPERIMENT – 15

AIM : To generate rectangular ,hamming ,hanning ,blackman and kaier window using MATLAB.

PROGRAM :

```
clc;
clear all;
n= input('order =');
x1 = hann(n);
x2 = hamming(n);
x3 = bartlett(n);
x4 = blackman(n);
x5 = triang(n);
x6 = kaiser(n);
plot(x1);
hold on;
grid on;
plot(x2,'*');
plot(x3,'.');
plot(x4,'x');
plot(x5,'+');
plot(x6,'^');
```

INPUT :

Order = 60

GRAPH :

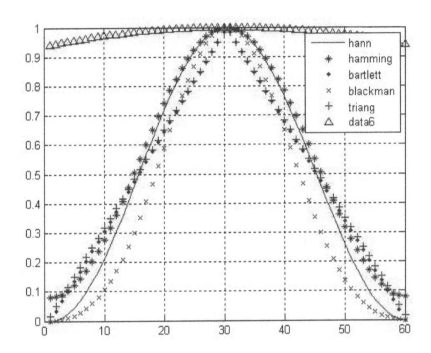

CONCLUSION :
From this experiment we can generate rectangular , hamming , hanning , blackman and kaier window using MATLAB.

DIGITAL SIGNAL PROCESSING

EXPERIMENT – 16

AIM : To design low pass filter using the Kaiser window using MATLAB.

PROGRAM :

```
clc;
clear all;
fpts=input('Type in the bandedges = ');
mag=input('Type in the desired magnitude values = ');
dev=input('Type in the ripples in each band = ');
type=input('Type in the sampling frequency = ');

[n,wn,beta,ftype]=kaiserord(fpts,mag,dev,type);
kw=kaiser(n+1,beta);
b=fir1(n,wn,kw);
[h,omega]=freqz(b,1,512);

plot(omega/pi,20*log10(abs(h)));
grid;
xlabel('\omega/\pi');
ylabel('GAIN,dB');
```

INPUT ;
Type in the bandedges = [1500 2000]
Type in the desired magnitude values = [1 0]
Type in the ripples in each band = [0.01 0.1]
Type in the sampling frequency = 8000

OUTPUT :

n = 36
Wn = 0.4375
beta = 3.3953
ftype = low

34

GRAPH :

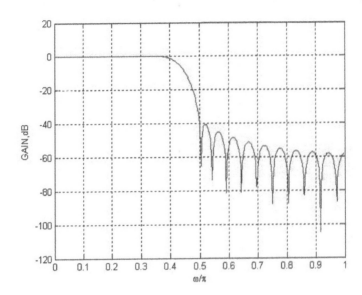

CONCLUSION :

By performing this experiment we can design low pass filter using the
Kaiser window using MATLAB.

EXPERIMENT – 17

AIM : To study coefficient quantization effects on the frequency response of a cascade form IIR filter using MATLAB.

PROGRAM :

```
clc;
clear all;
[z,p,k]=ellip(5,0.4,50,0.4);
[b,a]=zp2tf(z,p,k);
bq=roundn(b,-2);
aq=roundn(a,-2);
[h,w]=freqz(b,a,512);
g=20*log10(abs(h));
[hq,w]=freqz(bq,aq,512);
gq=20*log10(abs(hq));
plot(g);
hold on;
plot(gq,'r');
grid on;
```

GRAPH :

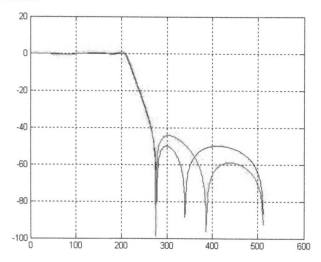

DIGITAL SIGNAL PROCESSING

CONCLUSION :
From this experiment we can study coefficient quantization effects on the
frequency response of a cascade form IIR filter using MATLAB.

www.ingramcontent.com/pod-product-compliance
Lightning Source LLC
LaVergne TN
LVHW042303060326
832902LV00009B/1233